Essential Insights from the spiritual writings of Bahá'u'lláh, 'Abdu'l-Bahá and Shoghi Effendi.

Mindfulness

Compiled and designed by Corinne Randall

To Masoud Yazdani, whose vision inspired the creation of these books,
you will always be in our hearts.

Meditation

Meditation is the key for opening the doors of mysteries.

In that state man abstracts himself: in that state man withdraws himself from all outside objects; in that subjective mood he is immersed in the ocean of spiritual life and can unfold the secrets of things-in-themselves.

To illustrate this, think of man as endowed with two kinds of sight; when the power of insight is being used the outward power of vision does not see.

'Abdu'l-Bahá

I now assure thee, O servant of God, that, if thy mind become empty and pure from every mention and thought and thy heart attracted wholly to the Kingdom of God, forget all else besides God and come in communion with the Spirit of God, then the Holy Spirit will assist thee with a power which will enable thee to penetrate all things, and a Dazzling Spark which enlightens all sides, a Brilliant Flame in the zenith of the heavens, will teach thee that which thou dost not know of the facts of the universe and of the divine doctrine.

'Abdu'l-Bahá

There is a sign from God in every phenomenon: the sign of the intellect is contemplation and the sign of contemplation is silence, because it is impossible for a man to do two things at one time—he cannot both speak and meditate.

It is an axiomatic fact that while you meditate you are speaking with your own spirit. In that state of mind you put certain questions to your spirit and the spirit answers: the light breaks forth and the reality is revealed. You cannot apply the name 'man' to any being void of this faculty of meditation; without it he would be a mere animal, lower than the beasts.

The meditative faculty is akin to the mirror; if you put it before earthly objects it will reflect them. Therefore if the spirit of man is contemplating earthly subjects he will be informed of these. But if you turn the mirror of your spirits heavenwards, the heavenly constellations and the rays of the Sun of Reality will be reflected in your hearts, and the virtues of the Kingdom will be obtained.

'Abdu'l-Bahá

O SON OF BEING!

Thy heart is my home; sanctify it for My descent. Thy spirit is My place of revelation; cleanse it for My manifestation.

O SON OF LIGHT!

Forget all save Me and commune with My spirit. This is of the essence of My command, therefore turn unto it.

Bahá'u'lláh

Close one eye and open the other.
Close one to the world and all that is therein,
and open the other to the hallowed
beauty of the Beloved.

Bahá'u'lláh

At every stage long ye for non-existence;
for when the ray returneth to the sun, it is wiped out,
and when the drop cometh to the sea, it vanisheth,
and when the true lover findeth his Beloved,
he yieldeth up his soul.

'Abdu'l-Bahá

Prayer

There is nothing sweeter in the world of existence than prayer. Man must live in a state of prayer. The most blessed condition is the condition of prayer and supplication. Prayer is conversation with God. The greatest attainment or the sweetest state is none other than conversation with God. It creates spirituality, creates mindfulness and celestial feelings, begets new attractions of the Kingdom and engenders the susceptibilities of the higher intelligence.

'Abdu'l-Bahá

If we wish to pray, we must have some object on which to concentrate. If we turn to God, we must direct our hearts to a certain centre.

If man worships God otherwise than through His Manifestation, he must first form a conception of God, and that conception is created by his own mind. As the finite cannot comprehend the Infinite, so God is not to be comprehended in this fashion.

If a man wishes to know God, he must find Him in the perfect mirror, Christ or Bahá'u'lláh (or the other Manifestations of God). In any of these mirrors he will see reflected the Sun of Divinity.

'Abdu'l-Bahá

In the highest prayer, men pray only for the love of God, not because they fear Him or hell, or hope for bounty or heaven…

The spiritual man finds no delight in anything save in commemoration of God.

If one friend loves another, is it not natural that he should wish to say so? Though he knows that that friend is aware of his love, does he still not wish to tell him of it?.. It is true that God knows the wishes of all hearts; but the impulse to pray is a natural one, springing from man's love to God.

Every joy is earthly save this one, the sweetness of which is divine.

'Abdu'l-Bahá

Reveal thyself, O Lord, by Thy merciful utterance and the mystery of Thy divine being, that the holy ecstacy of prayer may fill our souls – a prayer that shall rise above words and letters and transcend the murmur of syllables and sounds – that all things may be merged into nothingness before the revelation of Thy splendor.

'Abdu'l-Bahá

*God will answer the prayer of every
servant if that prayer is urgent.*

*His mercy is vast, illimitable.
He answers the prayers of all his servants.*

*He answers the prayer of this plant.
The plant prays potentially,
'O God! Send me rain!' God answers
the prayer, and the plant grows.*

God will answer anyone.

'Abdu'l-Bahá

Those who have passed on through death have a sphere of their own. It is not removed from ours: their work of the Kingdom, is ours; but it is sanctified from time and place. Time with us is measured by the sun. When there is no more sunrise, and no more sunset, that kind of time does not exist for man. Those who have ascended have different attributes (conditions) from those who are still on earth, yet there is no real separation. In prayer there is a mingling of stations, a mingling of condition. Pray for them as they pray for you.

'Abdu'l-Bahá

Intone, O My servant, the verses of God that have been received by thee, as intoned by them who have drawn nigh unto Him, that the sweetness of thy melody may kindle thine own soul, and attract the hearts of all men. Whoso reciteth, in the privacy of his chamber, the verses revealed by God, the scattering angels of the Almighty shall scatter abroad the fragrance of the words uttered by his mouth, and shall cause the heart of every righteous man to throb. Though he may, at first, remain unaware of its effect, yet the virtue of the grace vouchsafed unto him must needs sooner or later exercise its influence upon his soul.

Bahá'u'lláh

Prayer and fasting is the cause of awakening and mindfulness and conducive to protection and preservation from tests.

'Abdu'l-Bahá

Whensoever the light of Manifestation of the King of Oneness settleth upon the throne of the heart and soul, His shining becometh visible in every limb and member. At that time the mystery of the famed tradition gleameth out of the darkness: "A servant is drawn unto Me in prayer until I answer him; and when I have answered him, I become the ear wherewith he heareth…." For thus the Master of the house hath appeared within His home, and all the pillars of the dwelling are ashine with His light. And the action and effect of the light are from the Light-Giver; so it is that all move through Him and arise by His will.

Bahá'u'lláh

The most acceptable prayer is
the one offered with the utmost
spirituality and radiance;
its prolongation hath not been
and is not beloved by God.

The more detached and the purer
the prayer, the more acceptable
is it in the presence of God.

The Bab

*Prayer is both attitude and word...
It is like a song; both the words and music
make the song. Sometimes the melody will
move us, sometimes the words.*

*The state of prayer is the best of conditions,
for man is then associating with God.
Prayer verily bestoweth life, particularly
when offered in private and at times, such as
midnight, when freed from daily cares.*

'Abdu'l-Bahá

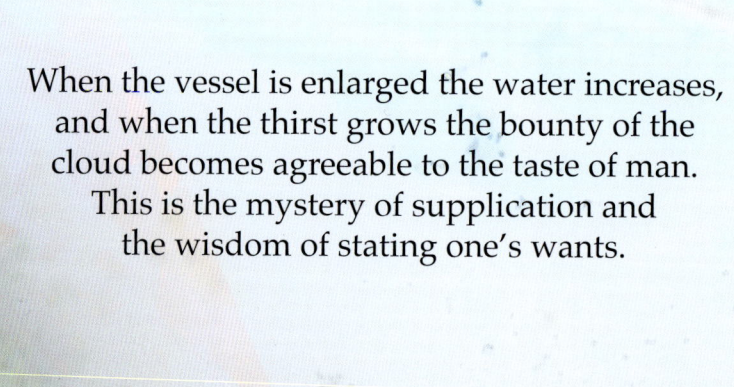

When the vessel is enlarged the water increases, and when the thirst grows the bounty of the cloud becomes agreeable to the taste of man. This is the mystery of supplication and the wisdom of stating one's wants.

'Abdu'l-Bahá

A divine Mine only can yield
the gems of divine knowledge,
and the fragrance of the mystic Flower
can be inhaled only in the ideal Garden,
and the lilies of ancient wisdom
can blossom nowhere except in
the city of a stainless heart.

Bahá'u'lláh

The blessings of Bahá'u'lláh are a shoreless sea, and even life everlasting is only a dewdrop therefrom. The waves of that sea are continually lapping against the hearts of the friends, and from those waves there come intimations of the spirit and ardent pulsings of the soul, until the heart giveth way, and willing or not, turneth humbly in prayer unto the Kingdom of the Lord.

'Abdu'l-Bahá

O my brother! Take thou the step of the spirit, so that, swift as the twinkling of an eye, thou mayest flash through the wilds of remoteness and bereavement, attain the Ridván of everlasting reunion, and in one breath commune with the heavenly Spirits. For with human feet thou canst never hope to traverse these immeasurable distances, nor attain thy goal.

Bahá'u'lláh

Becoming Mindful

Greater than the prayer is the spirit in which it is uttered and greater than the way it is uttered is the spirit in which it is carried out.

Shoghi Effendi

Their outward conduct is but a reflection of their inward life, and their inward life a mirror of their outward conduct.

Bahá'u'lláh

*Man is eternally in a state of communion
and prayer with the source of all good.*

'Abdu'l-Bahá

*You are always in the Presence of God.
Open the windows of your soul
so His Presence may be within you.*

'Abdu'l-Bahá

Beware! Beware!
Lest ye offend any heart!

Beware! Beware!
Lest ye hurt any soul!

Beware! Beware!
Lest ye deal unkindly toward any person!

Beware! Beware!
Lest ye be the cause of hopelessness to any creature!

'Abdu'l-Bahá

*Let each morn be better than its eve
and each morrow richer than its yesterday.*

Bahá'u'lláh

*Faith is the magnet which draws the
confirmations of the Merciful One.
Service is the magnet which attracts
the heavenly strength.*

'Abdu'l-Bahá

All effort and exertion put forth by man from the fullness of his heart is worship, if it is prompted by the highest motives and the will to do service to humanity.

*Prayer need not be in words,
but rather in thought and attitude.*

*Strive that your actions day by day
may be beautiful prayers.*

'Abdu'l-Bahá

Dynamics of Prayer for Solving Problems.

First Step: *Pray and meditate about it. Use the prayers of the Manifestations as they have the greatest power. Then remain in the silence of contemplation for a few minutes.*

Second Step: *Arrive at a decision and hold this. This decision is usually born during the contemplation. It may seem almost impossible of accomplishment but if it seems to be as answer to a prayer or a way of solving the problem, then immediately take the next step.*

Third Step: *Have determination to carry the decision through. Many fail here. The decision, budding into determination, is blighted and instead becomes a wish or a vague longing. When determination is born, immediately take the next step.*

Fourth Step: *Have faith and confidence that the power will flow through you, the right way will appear, the door will open, the right thought, the right message, the right principle or the right book will be given you. Have confidence, and the right thing will come to your need. Then, as you rise from prayer, take at once the fifth step.*

Fifth Step: *Act as though it had all been answered. Act with tireless, ceaseless energy. And as you act, you, yourself, will become a magnet, which will attract more power to your being, until you become an unobstructed channel for the Divine power to flow through you.*

Many pray but do not remain for the last half of the first step. Some who meditate arrive at a decision, but fail to hold it. Few have the determination to carry the decision through, still fewer have the confidence that the right thing will come to their need. But how many remember to act as though it had all been answered? How true are those words – "Greater than the prayer is the spirit in which it is uttered" and greater than the way it is uttered is the spirit in which it is carried out.

Shoghi Effendi (Pilgrim's notes)

REFERENCES

p. 3.	'Abdu'l-Bahá, *Paris Talks*, UK Bahá'í Publishing Trust, 1972, p.175
p. 5.	'Abdu'l-Bahá, *Tablets of 'Abdu'l-Bahá 'Abbas*, Bahá'í Publishing Committee, 1909, pp.706-707
p. 6.	'Abdu'l-Bahá, *Paris Talks,* UK Bahá'í Publishing Trust, 1972, p.174
p. 7.	*ibid,* p.176
p. 8.	Bahá'u'lláh, *The Hidden Words*, no. 59 from the Arabic.
p. 9.	*ibid,* No.16 from the Arabic.
p. 11a	Bahá'u'lláh, *The Hidden Words*, no.12 from the Persian.
p. 11b	'Abdu'l-Bahá, *Selections from the Writings of 'Abdu'l-Bahá*, Bahá'í World Centre, 1982, p.76
p. 13.	'Abdu'l-Bahá, cited in *Star of the West,* vol VIII, No.4, 17 May 1917, p.41
p. 15.	'Abdu'l-Bahá, quoted in *Bahá'u'lláh and the New Era*, J.E. Esslemont, US Bahá'í Publishing Trust, 1980. p.91
p. 16a	'Abdu'l-Bahá, quoted in *Bahá'u'lláh and the New Era*, J.E. Esslemont, US Bahá'í Publishing Trust, 1980, p.94-5
p. 16b	*ibid,* p.94
p. 17a	*ibid,* p.94
p. 17b	'Abdu'l-Bahá, *The Importance of Obligatory Prayer and Fasting,* UK Bahá'í Publishing Trust, 2000, p.11
p. 19.	'Abdu'l-Bahá, *Bahá'í Prayers*, US Bahá'í Publishing Trust, 1991, p.70-1
p. 21.	'Abdu'l-Bahá, *The Promulgation of Universal Peace,* US Bahá'í Publishing Trust, 1982, p.246
p. 23.	'Abdu'l-Bahá, *'Abdu'l-Bahá in London,* UK Bahá'í Publishing Trust, 1982 reprint, p.96
p. 25.	Bahá'u'lláh, *Bahá'í Prayers,* US Bahá'í Publishing Trust, 1991, p.iv
p. 26.	'Abdu'l-Bahá, *Tablets of 'Abdu'l-Bahá 'Abbas*, Bahá'í Publishing Committee, 1909, pp.684

p. 27.	Bahá'u'lláh, *The Seven Valleys and The Four Valleys*, US Bahá'í Publishing Trust, 1991, pocket-size edition, p.22
p. 29.	The Báb, *Selections from the Writings of The Báb*, Bahá'í World Centre, 1982, lightweight edition. p.78
p. 31a	'Abdu'l-Bahá, *Ten Days in the Light of Akka*, Julia M. Grundy, 1907 pp.15-20. (www.cerrato.se/tendays)
p. 31b	'Abdu'l-Bahá, *Selections from the Writings of 'Abdu'l-Bahá*, p.202
p. 32.	'Abdu'l-Bahá, quoted in *Bahá'u'lláh and the New Era*, J.E. Esslemont, US Bahá'í Publishing Trust, 1980. p.89
p. 33.	Bahá'u'lláh, *Kitáb-i-Iqán*, p.122
p. 35.	'Abdu'l-Bahá, *Selections from the Writings of 'Abdu'l-Bahá*, pp.192-3
p. 37.	Bahá'u'lláh, *Kitáb-i-Íqán*, London: Bahá'í Publishing Trust, 1982, p.28
p. 38a	Shoghi Effendi, *'Pilgrim's notes'*, *Baha'i Prayers and Holy Writings*. pp.127, Bahá'í Publishing Trust of the Spiritual Assembly of the Bahá'ís of Malaysia.
p. 38b	Bahá'u'lláh, *Gleanings from the Writings of Bahá'u'lláh*. US Baha'i Publishing Trust, 1990 pocket-size edition, p.271
p. 39a	'Abdu'l-Bahá, quoted in *Do'a* by Ruth Moffett, 1933, p.77 (*Star of the West*, volume 8, issue 4)
p. 39b	'Abdu'l-Bahá, *Ten days in the Light of Akka*, Julia M. Grundy, 1907 p.40-3
p. 40.	'Abdu'l-Bahá, quoted in *Bahá'u'lláh and the New Era*, J.E. Esslemont, US Bahá'í Publishing Trust, 1980. p.81
p. 41a	Bahá'u'lláh, *Tablets of Bahá'u'lláh revealed after the Kitáb-i-Aqdas*, 1988, pocket-size edition, p.138
p. 41b	'Abdu'l-Bahá, *Tablets of 'Abdu'l-Bahá 'Abbas*, Bahá'í Publishing Committee, 1909, p.62
p. 42.	'Abdu'l-Bahá, *Paris Talks*, UK Bahá'í Publishing Trust, 1972, p.175
p. 43.	'Abdu'l-Bahá, quoted in *Bahá'u'lláh and the New Era*, J.E. Esslemont, p.25
pp. 44-5.	Shoghi Effendi, *'Pilgrim's notes'*, *Baha'i Prayers and Holy Writings*, Bahá'í Publishing Trust, Malaysia, pp.126-7

First Published in the UK in 2014 by
Intellect, The Mill, Parnall Road, Fishponds, Bristol, BS16 3JG, UK

First published in the USA in 2014
by Intellect, The University of Chicago Press, 1427 E. 60th Street, Chicago, IL 60637, USA

Copyright © 2014 Intellect Ltd

All rights reserved. No part of this publication may be reproduced, stored in a retrieval system, or transmitted, in any form or by any means, electronic, mechanical, photocopying, recording, or otherwise, without written permission.

A catalogue record for this book is available from the British Library.

Book Design: Corinne Randall
Publisher: Masoud Yazdani
ISBN: 978-1-78320-098-6
Printed and bound by Gomer Press Ltd.

Other books in the *Essential Insights* series.
Healing, Truthfulness, Detachment, Openness, Oneness, Generosity, Gratefulness, Love, Simplicity, Awareness, Transformation.